museum **highlights**

A Pool of London docker, 1947
This view is of a docker handling a cargo
of bagged nuts craned up from the gaping
holds below, and was taken towards
Tower Bridge from approximately the
present position of City Hall.
PLA Collection photograph.

CONTENTS

Limehouse Reach **(detail), 1798, William Anderson**
This aquatint shows the westward side of the Isle of Dogs. The line of windmills can be seen clearly. They gave the area its name – Millwall. In the foreground, two men are fishing from a peterboat with a 20-gun naval vessel beyond.

FOREWORD

Welcome to the Museum of London Docklands.

The building you are standing in is an early nineteenth-century sugar warehouse. Its resonant atmosphere makes it the perfect place to tell the stories of trade, migration and commerce you will find in this Museum. It is a surviving testament to London's commercial past, including the city's involvement with slavery.

London has always been a place of trade. From Roman settlement to today's Docklands, the city has drawn its strength from the movement of people and commodities around the world. By the nineteenth century, London's port complex was the largest in the world; and with sea-borne trade came people and a new cosmopolitan flavour to London's East End.

The 11 permanent galleries in the Museum tell the story of the local communities in London's East End riversides. But the story is not just a local one. The award-winning *London, Sugar and Slavery* gallery explores London's part in the 'West India Trade', whose tentacles stretched from the Caribbean islands to Africa. The Sainsbury Study Centre encourages access to important business archives that recount the history of one of the UK's best-known food retailers from its foundation in Victorian London, the Port and River Library and Archives, and the Museum's slavery-related archive.

I hope you will find much more to enjoy and reflect on whilst you are here.

Professor Jack Lohman
Director, Museum of London

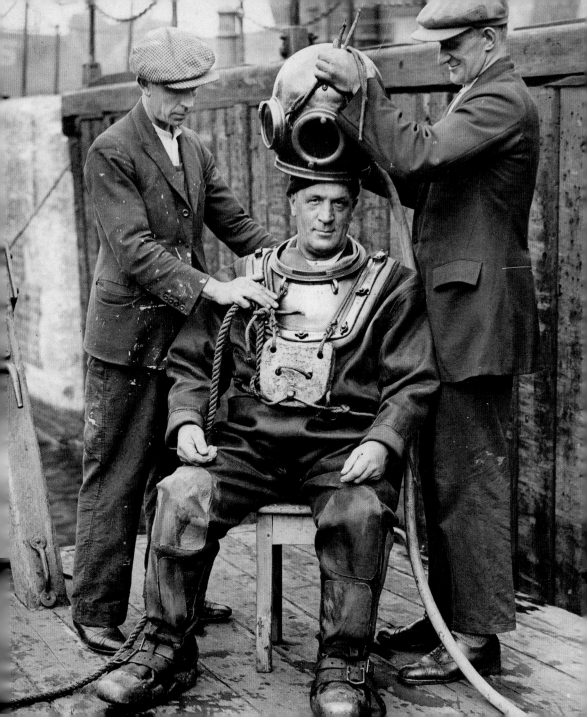

THE BUILDING

The Museum occupies three of the five bays of No.1 Warehouse, West India Quay. The West India Docks were completed in 1802 following the passing of the West India Dock Act of 1799. The Act enabled the West India merchants and plantation owners in London to raise private funding to build docks and warehouses to handle the valuable produce of Britain's slave plantations in the Caribbean. The dock basin outside was used by ships operating in the Triangle Trade: sailing from here to West Africa to barter for enslaved Africans and carrying them in terrible conditions to the Caribbean to be sold into plantation slavery. The same ships returned to this dock with their cargoes, thus completing the 'Triangle'.

The building was heightened in 1827 to make room for goods produced in the East Indies and until 1883 the building was one of London's largest tea warehouses. The westernmost bay of the building was used to house ships' stores and passengers' baggage.

The building survived a fire in 1901 and the Blitz of September 1940, which destroyed all but Warehouses 1 and 2. The West India Docks closed in 1980. Derelict for many years, the building was Grade-1 listed before being acquired and converted for use as a museum between 1999–2003.

RIVER, PORT AND PEOPLE

The galleries of the Museum of London Docklands trace the fascinating 2,000-year story of London's river, port and people. It is a story that stretches from the arrival of the Romans to the rise of Canary Wharf. In this introductory gallery, TV historian Tony Robinson outlines the importance of the Thames to London throughout history. Taking his view from the historic City foreshore and the Canary Wharf Tower, Robinson emphasises the role of the river in facilitating the movement of people and the development of trade. Without the river, there would be no London.

Limehouse, **1859, James Abbott McNeill Whistler**
The etching shows Broadway Wharf with the Old Harbour Master's House on the right.

Gun Wharves, 1937
This is a section from a
Port of London Authority
commissioned
photographic panorama of
both banks of the River
Thames from London Bridge
to Greenwich/Island
Gardens.

**View across the River
Thames of Canary Wharf,
2009**
The dramatic skyline of
Canary Wharf now
dominates the Isle of Dogs.
Photograph by John Chase.

THAMES HIGHWAY AD43–1600

The story begins around AD50, with the Roman settlement in what is now the City of London. As early as AD61, Tacitus, the Roman senator and historian described London as 'an important centre for merchants'. Luxury and utilitarian cargoes came from across the Roman Empire. London exported grain, hides, metals and slaves. The Roman troops withdrew in AD410, and the Anglo-Saxon settlers avoided the old Roman walled city. By AD600, the Saxon settlement of 'Lundenwic' was well established, with a beach market along the line of the present day Aldwych and the Strand. The scholar monk, Bede, described it as 'the mart of many nations'. Attacked by Vikings, the Saxons abandoned the settlement in favour of the old walled city around AD886. New beach markets lined the waterfront of 'Lundenburgh' east and west of a timber bridge.

Baltic amber beads, 1066–1480
These beads were imported into London for jewellery and decoration.

Roman barrel lid, AD50–70
Made from Lebanese cedarwood, the barrel was coated in pitch to protect its contents during the journey to Londinium.

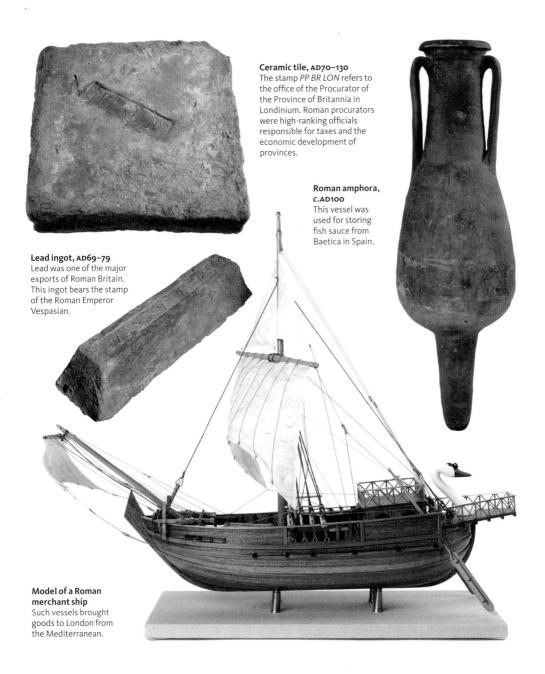

Ceramic tile, AD70–130
The stamp *PP BR LON* refers to the office of the Procurator of the Province of Britannia in Londinium. Roman procurators were high-ranking officials responsible for taxes and the economic development of provinces.

Roman amphora, c.AD100
This vessel was used for storing fish sauce from Baetica in Spain.

Lead ingot, AD69–79
Lead was one of the major exports of Roman Britain. This ingot bears the stamp of the Roman Emperor Vespasian.

Model of a Roman merchant ship
Such vessels brought goods to London from the Mediterranean.

Between 1176 and 1209, the City built a massive new stone London Bridge. The waterfront was successively embanked between 1200 and 1500. In 1389, the City became responsible for managing the river between Staines and the Medway, including its fish stocks. In 1559, 21 Legal Quays were established on the City waterfront, for the handling of all dutiable cargoes. After 1550, groups of merchant venturers reaped the combined benefits of protective trading monopolies, a stronger navy and declining European ports. In 1566, Thomas Gresham founded a meeting house for merchants in Cornhill; it became the Royal Exchange in 1571. By the 1590s, trade expansion had resulted in the rapid development of riverside communities east of the City.

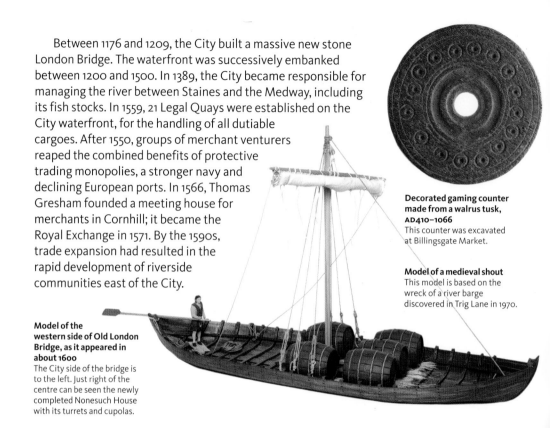

Decorated gaming counter made from a walrus tusk, AD410–1066
This counter was excavated at Billingsgate Market.

Model of a medieval shout
This model is based on the wreck of a river barge discovered in Trig Lane in 1970.

Model of the western side of Old London Bridge, as it appeared in about 1600
The City side of the bridge is to the left. Just right of the centre can be seen the newly completed Nonesuch House with its turrets and cupolas.

**Inscribed bone handle,
AD410–1066**
Boneworking was one
of many crafts practised
in the Saxon port of
Lundenwic.

Pilgrim badge, 14th century
The area near London Bridge was
often the starting point for
pilgrimages to shrines such as
St Thomas in Canterbury and
St Peter's in Rome. This badge in
the shape of a scallop shell is of
St James of Compostella.

**Jug made in Saintogne,
France, 1266–1335**
Great quantities of wine
were imported into London
from Bordeaux at this time.
This jug reflects this
extensive trade.

**Pilgrim badge,
14th century**
This is a souvenir
brought back to London
of Our Lady of the Sea, a
famous statue in the
cathdral at Boulogne.

TRADE EXPANSION 1600–1800

Developments in shipbuilding, seamanship and navigational knowledge helped the growth of Britain's overseas interests. Protected by an increasingly powerful navy, Britain challenged her European rivals for trade and territory. International expansion was mirrored in the growth of London, its population and its port activities.

The largest ships dominated trade with the East and West Indies, North America, the Baltic and the Mediterranean. Between 1600 and 1798, the number of coastal and overseas ships using London rose from 3,000 to 14,600. The business of the port was transacted in City coffee houses, the Royal Exchange and merchants' counting houses. The most valuable cargoes were handled at the Legal Quays, between London Bridge and the Tower. As port trade increased in the eighteenth century, HM Customs allowed 'Sufferance Wharves' on the Bermondsey and St Katharine's waterfronts. Only the smaller ships could discharge directly at these quays and wharves.

Wrought iron gibbet cage used to hold the corpses of executed felons, 18th century
The spectacle of rotting bodies in such cages along the banks of the River Thames acted as a warning to sailors against criminal acts.

Silver waterman's badge, 1763
Made by Benjamin Gignac and bearing the coat of arms of the East India Company, 1763.

The Inside of the Royal Exchange in London, **1788, engraving by Francesco Bartolozzi**

Part of the Legal Quay reconstruction, *c.*1790
The windows of a small counting house can be seen where a wharfinger or wharf operator would have worked. Cargo-handling equipment displayed includes a large beamscale on the left which was used to weigh cargoes.

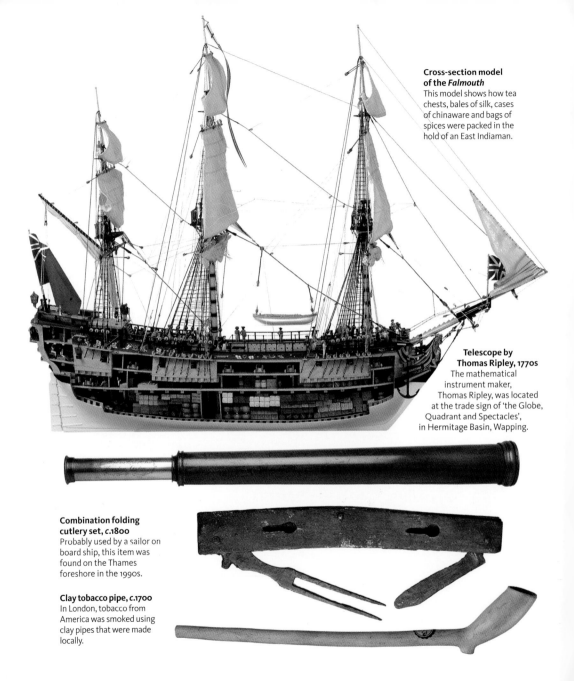

Cross-section model of the *Falmouth*
This model shows how tea chests, bales of silk, cases of chinaware and bags of spices were packed in the hold of an East Indiaman.

Telescope by Thomas Ripley, 1770s
The mathematical instrument maker, Thomas Ripley, was located at the trade sign of 'the Globe, Quadrant and Spectacles', in Hermitage Basin, Wapping.

Combination folding cutlery set, *c.*1800
Probably used by a sailor on board ship, this item was found on the Thames foreshore in the 1990s.

Clay tobacco pipe, *c.*1700
In London, tobacco from America was smoked using clay pipes that were made locally.

Wooden tillet block, 1775–1820
This was used to print identification marks onto coarse cloth to protect bales of textiles for export.

Iron padlock inscribed with the arms of the East India Company, 1775–1820
Such padlocks would have been used to secure cargo hatches on lighters and hoys.

Sailmakers' seam rubbers, 19th century
Made of bone and wood, these hand tools were used to produce sharp folds in the sail canvas prior to sewing.

Stone fragment, *c.*1618
Carved with the lower half of the Coat of Arms of the East India Company, this was probably placed over the main gateway of the company's shipyard at Blackwall.

Silver Admiralty waterman's badge, 1746, made by Nicholas Sprimont

Isaac Hildrup's Billingsgate Fellowship porter's licence, 1769
Attached to the brass licence is a leather panel with pierced leather tallies, on which different jobs undertaken by the porter could be recorded by cord thongs. The Fellowship of Billingsgate Porters were licensed by the City Corporation to handle measurable cargoes such as grain, malt, salt, fish, fruit and vegetables.

Carved wooden ship's figurehead representing Pocahontas or the *Indian Queen*, 19th century

Flintlock muzzle loading gun, 1750–1830
This gun was used in a warehouse in Tower Street to deter thieves from trying to enter and steal cargo.

Shop sign, *c*.1740
The relief carving is of two fishermen in a double-ended peterboat with anchor, net and fish in the centre of the boat. At the top of the cartouche is a carving of a doublet. The sign hung outside the shop premises of William Good & Son, rope and twine makers, 46 Fish Street Hill.

Tin-glazed ceramic tea bowl made in Lambeth, late 17th century
The decoration around the bowl was inspired by Chinese porcelain.

Chinese porcelain soup bowl, 1751–1800
This soup bowl carries the arms of the Fishmongers' Company.

Small wine glass, *c*.1762
The glass is engraved with a ship and the inscription 'Success to ye Ld Clive'. The *Lord Clive* was an East India Company ship.

LONDON, SUGAR AND SLAVERY 1600 ONWARDS

Until comparatively recently, London's role in the transatlantic slave trade had been forgotten. Within the last few years, research by a transatlantic team of scholars has revealed once again the extent of London's involvement in this wicked trade. It is now realised that London was the fourth most important slave trading port in the world. Only ships registered in Liverpool, and Bahia and Rio in South America, carried more African men, women and children into slavery.

London, however, benefited more than any of those ports from the profits of slavery. Money raised from the sale of the enslaved or the sugar and rum they produced, found its way into the commercial world of the capital, into banks and finance houses, insurance, shipbuilding, government contracting, convict transportation, and other trades like the East Indies and Baltic trades, whaling and dock building.

Thomas King entering London Dock, 1827, **William John Huggins**
This painting, looking north, shows the wharves and buildings on either side of the Wapping Entrance.

Gold and oak snuffbox, 1810
On the lid is an engraving of the *Henry Addington*, the ship which formally opened the West India Dock in August 1802.

Red earthenware sugar mould, c.1670
Sugar from the West Indies was processed in London refineries and formed into sugar 'loaves' or cones using such moulds.

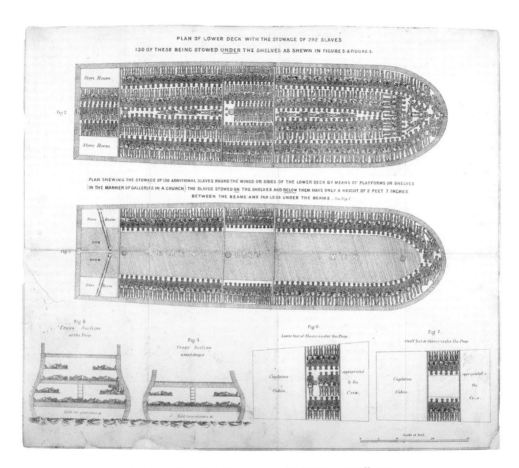

PLAN OF LOWER DECK WITH THE STOWAGE OF 292 SLAVES
130 OF THESE BEING STOWED UNDER THE SHELVES AS SHEWN IN FIGURE 5 & FIGURE 3.

PLAN SHEWING THE STOWAGE OF 130 ADDITIONAL SLAVES ROUND THE WINGS OR SIDES OF THE LOWER DECK BY MEANS OF PLATFORMS OR SHELVES (IN THE MANNER OF GALLERIES IN A CHURCH) THE SLAVES STOWED ON THE SHELVES AND BELOW THEM HAVE ONLY A HEIGHT OF 2 FEET 7 INCHES BETWEEN THE BEAMS: AND FAR LESS UNDER THE BEAMS. See Fig 1.

The Liverpool slave ship *Brookes*, 1789
Produced by the abolition committee to illustrate the inhumane conditions on slave ships, this print was widely circulated.

Dock policeman's tipstaff, 1802
Presented to Captain Bartlett on his appointment as Captain of the Watch and Head Constable for the West India Dock Company.

**The Fruits of
Early Industry
and Economy**, 1789,
**after a painting by
George Morland**
All the rewards of
mercantile hard
work and 'industry'
are shown here,
including an
African 'servant'.

Guinea, 1686
Minted from African gold
imported from the Guinea
coast of West Africa by 'the
company of Royal Adventurers
of England trading into Africa'.

George Hibbert, 1811,
Sir Thomas Lawrence
Hibbert was chairman of the
West India Dock Company
and opposed the abolition of
the slave trade on which his
wealth and power depended.

**The actor Lloyd Gordon
in the role of the
revolutionary preacher
Robert Wedderburn**
This photograph by Paul
Howard is a satirical echo of
the George Hibbert portrait.

The City of Loango,
18th century
The engraving by G. Child
shows the capital city of the
African kingdom of Loango,
now in the Republic of Congo,
which thrived between the
15th and 19th centuries.

English Castle at
Anamabou, 18th century
This English settlement,
in what is now Ghana,
was established by the
Royal Africa Company in
1679 to trade in slaves
and gold.

The Mills Papers

In 2006, the Museum acquired a collection of manuscript papers produced by Thomas and John Mills, London merchants and owners of plantations in St Kitts and Nevis. The papers consist of Letter Books, journals of day-to-day work on the plantations and details of the enslaved workforce. The papers open a fascinating yet chilling window into the lives of both enslaved and enslavers in the 1760s–70s.

Some of the papers are on display in the gallery. They include a letter illustrating the Mills's involvement in the slave trade; references to brutality on their plantation; and paradoxically, a copy of a personal letter written by the plantation owner to one of his enslaved men – revealing a relationship beyond that of slave and slave owner. Facsimile copies of the papers are available for researchers by appointment in the Sainsbury Study Centre on the first floor of the Museum.

Flagellation of a Female Samboe Slave, **1796, William Blake**
This engraving was used in the abolition campaign to highlight the cruelty of slave owners.

Slave Trade, **1791**
Engraving by J.R. Smith after the painting by George Morland.

OPPOSITE:
A plantation inventory, 1777
The list of enslaved Africans includes boys, girls and very young children, some no more than a few months old.

No	NAMES	Employment	Age	Condition	NAMES	Employment	Age	Condition
80	brought	over			118 brought	forward		
81	Lucy	infield		healthy	119 Nanny	in field		healthy
82	Sukey	ditto		ditto	120 Nelly mills	ditto		ditto
83	Sylvia	ditto		ditto	121 Nelly Little	ditto		ditto
84	Sophia	ditto		ditto	122 Patefield	ditto		ditto
85	Statira	ditto		ditto	123 Penelopa	ditto		ditto
86	Lucy Brown	ditto		ditto	124 Sarah	ditto		ditto
87	Susannah	ditto	stout	ditto	125 Sarah Little	ditto		ditto
88	Venus	ditto		ditto	126 Sally mill	ditto		ditto
	Boys				127 Vernor	ditto		ditto
89	Burgandy	ditto		ditto	128 Violet	ditto		ditto
90	Bridgwater	ditto		ditto	Children		years	Months old
91	Constant	ditto		ditto	129 Andrew Little		1	10
92	Comey	ditto		ditto	130 Billy		5	
93	Hero	ditto		ditto	131 Cæsar		6	
94	Jacob	in house		ditto	132 Cudgo		1	3
95	Jupiter	infield		ditto	133 Catto	born augt 16th 1776		10
96	Neptune	ditto		ditto				
97	Newport	ditto		ditto	134 Dickey		4	
98	Peter	ditto		ditto	135 Fido		5	
99	Polido	imperfect with much	ditto		136 George Little		3	5
100	Richard	ditto with colds	ditto		137 Jackey		3	3
101	Saturday	infield		ditto	138 Nimble		3	6
102	Sharp	ditto		ditto	139 Sunday		5	
103	Tomey	overseer of small gang	ditto		140 Saunderson		6	
104	Jackey	in stable groom		ditto	141 Jet	born 24 1776		10
105	Toby	infield		ditto	142 Daniel	ditto sept 17th		9
106	Wakefield	ditto		ditto	143 Monday		5	
	Girls				144 Christmas	dat Decr 26		5
					145 Fido Little	ditto Janry 15 1777		4

Anti-slavery creamware sugar bowl, 1825
Painted on the back is the message 'East India Sugar not made by slaves. By six families using East India, instead of West India Sugar, one slave less is required'.

LEFT: *May Morning*, *c.1760*, John Collet

Medals commemorating the abolition of slavery, 1834

The eventual abolition of both the slave trade in 1807 and slavery itself was a colossal achievement, especially given the wealth and power that was interested in its continuation. While the parliamentary conclusion to those campaigns was focused in London, the movement towards abolition was based upon the perpetual and resolute resistance from the enslaved themselves, which helped undermine the profitability of slavery.

Whilst the abolition of slavery in 1833 resulted in a certain amount of righteous celebration, it also masked a new system of exploitation in the East Indies, which helped maintain Britain's military and trading empire. It also meant that the injustices of slavery and the racism it engendered remained unresolved and continue as a legacy for our society today.

Englishmen!

NEGRO APPRENTICESHIP

is proved to be but another name for

SLAVERY.

SIGN
TEN
WITHOUT DELAY
THE
PETITION
Lying within
FOR IMMEDIATE
ABOLITION

Portrait of Thomas Clarkson (detail), slavery abolitionist, engraving by Charles Turner after Alfred Edward Chalon.

Anti-apprenticeship banner, c.1833
Produced by campaigners bitterly opposed to the imposition of compulsory 'apprenticeship' on those liberated from slavery. *On loan from Anti-Slavery International.*

Calypso advertising figure, promoting the Caribbean rum trade, 1960–70

CITY AND RIVER 1800–1840

Parliament passed acts for the building of new trading docks east of the Tower. The West India Docks, which cut across the north of the Isle of Dogs, opened in 1802 and the London Docks, at Wapping, in 1805. In 1806, the East India Docks opened at Blackwal Between them, they enjoyed specific 21-year monopolies on most dutiable cargoes. The Legal Quays and Sufferance Wharves lost their privileges. The City Canal opened in 1805 to the south of the West India Docks. In Rotherhithe, new timber and grain handling docks were developed around the Greenland Dock. By 1810, London had the best port facilities in the world. St Katharine Docks opened as London's first purpose-built free trade dock in 1828. The forced clearance of the urban site east of the Tower raised social issues that were to echo through time to the Docklands' redevelopment of the 1980s.

The opening of John Rennie's new London Bridge in 1831, and the demolition of the old medieval one, drew another line between past and present. Wider bridge arches increased the flow of the river, consigning the picturesque frost fairs to the history books.

As well as new bridges over the Thames, Marc Isambard Brunel's workmen were busy beneath the riverbed, building the Thames Tunnel between Wapping and Rotherhithe. Constructed between 1825 and 1843, it was the world's first tunnel under a navigable waterway.

St Katharine Dock Company workers lead badge, c.1828
Such badges were worn by messengers, constables and gatekeepers employed by the dock company.

A View of the London Docks (detail), 1808, William Daniell
This aquatint looks eastwards, with the Isle of Dogs in the distance.

Log of the South Seas whaling ship, *Mary*, 1823–24
At the peak of its activity, the South Sea whaling fleet numbered 149 and, for a short while, London was the largest whaling port in the world. This log records whale kills with a black tail, whilst a smiling whale indicates a lost catch.

Scrimshaw, 1840–70
The engraving and decoration of whale teeth and bone began in the early 19th century as a pastime for sailors on whale ships who were often at sea for up to four years.

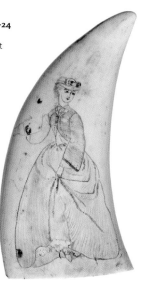

Hand harpoon
This was used onboard the *William and Ann*, a Leith Greenland whaling ship, in 1833.

Dock company weapons, 1830–50
Dock police were usually armed only with wooden truncheons. During times of civil unrest, however, they were issued with guns and swords.

Painted wherry seat back, 1824
This was awarded to the winner of the 6th Queenhithe watermen's race and includes a painted view of Southwark Bridge.

Model of a Thames skiff, c.1835
At this date, skiffs had begun to replace wherries, which were endangered by the wash of fast paddle steamers.

Souvenir paperweight, 1831–33
This paperweight is made from marble removed from the old London Bridge.

Circular steel seal
of The Company of Proprietors of the Waterloo Bridge, 1816.

A View of Frost Fair on the Thames, February 1814
Enterprising watermen who had been thrown out of work by the freezing of the Thames secured payment from the public by helping them down onto the ice.

A View of the Tunnel under the Thames, 1827

This peepshow, produced shortly before the works were flooded, gave a perspective view of how the tunnel would look when completed. The building of the Thames Tunnel enthralled Londoners and tourists. Many travelled down to view the works at Rotherhithe and Wapping, where they were able to purchase cheap souvenirs, such as this peepshow, to commemorate their visit.

SAILORTOWN 1840–1850

St Katharine's, Wapping, Shadwell, Ratcliffe, Limehouse, Poplar, Bermondsey, Rotherhithe, Deptford, Greenwich, Woolwich and Gravesend all catered for sailors. This was the land of 'Jack Ashore'. The most famous 'Sailortown' quarter encompassed Wapping, Shadwell and Ratcliffe Highway. A maze of streets, lanes and alleys backed the riverside wharves and docks. Here were to be found ship chandlers, curio sellers, slop sellers, sailors' lodging houses, alehouses, ginshops, brothels, slum houses, cook shops, wild animal shops and pawnshops.

Life En Passant, 1833–35
Illustration by Robert Cruikshank from the book *Finish to the Adventures of Tom, Jerry and Logic in their pursuits through Life in and out of London* by Pierce Egan.

OPPOSITE:
Ship chandlers
In every street and alley in the vicinity of the docks and river Thames there were ship chandlers. They supplied customers with all types of gear and fittings for ships including rope and pulley blocks.

FIRST PORT OF EMPIRE 1840–1880

London benefited enormously from its position as the trading heart of the British Empire. Between 1855 and 1886, a series of important new docks were opened to accommodate steamships. The progressive removal of selected customs duties, from the 1840s, encouraged the rebuilding of river wharves. The 'free water clause' enabled lighters to enter the docks free of charge. By the 1870s, the wharves were siphoning off around three-quarters of dock imports. The frustrations of many workers erupted during the 1889 Dock Strike. The creation of the Port of London Authority (PLA) in 1909 brought a much-needed rationalisation to port activities.

BELOW AND OPPOSITE:
***Tilbury Fort, Wind Against Tide*, 1849, Clarkson Stanfield**
This painting shows the hazards which small craft faced on the River Thames. Two fishermen in a peterboat are in peril of being struck by a Thames sailing barge, laden with hay, tacking directly at them. The work was painted for Robert Stephenson, the famous railway engineer and Member of Parliament.

The riverside east and west of the City attracted large-scale industry, including shipyards, engineering works, potteries, gasworks and soap and candleworks.

Iron shipbuilding and engine-making expanded rapidly in the 1840s and 1850s, at the Isle of Dogs, Bow Creek and Greenwich. Isambard Kingdom Brunel's Great Eastern was launched at John Scott Russell's Millwall Yard in 1858.

Billingsgate fish porter's hat, 1910–35
Also known as Bobbins, these leather hats had a flat, hardened top to support large rectangular boxes of fish and an upturned brim to protect the porter's head from dripping fish juices.

The Great Eastern on the Stocks, c.1857
Designed by Isambard Kingdom Brunel and John Scott Russell, this ship was built at Millwall and was the largest vessel afloat until she was broken up in 1888.

DOCK LABORERS' STRIKE.

ALGAMATED AND UNITED SOCIETIES OF STEVEDORES.

To the Trade Unionists and People of London.

FRIENDS AND FELLOW WORKMEN!

The DOCK LABORERS are on Strike, and are asking for an advance of wages—the wages they now receive being 5d. per hour day-time, and 6d. overtime. They now ask 6d. per hour day-time, and 8d. per hour overtime. The work is of the most precarious nature, three hours being the average amount per day obtained by the "docker." We, the Union Stevedores of London, knowing the condition of the Dock Laborers, have determined to support their movement by every lawful means in our power. We have, therefore, refused to work because of the Dock Co. employing scabs and blacklegs who are taking the places of the Dock Laborers on strike. We do this not to inconvenience the Brokers, Ship Owners, or Master Stevedores, as our quarrel is not with them; but we feel our duty is to support our poorer brothers. We are promised the help of the Seamen's & Firemen's Union, and we now appeal with confidence to Members of all Trade Unions for joint action with us, and especially those whose work is in connexion with Shipping, Sea-going Engineers and Fitters, Boilermakers, Ship Carpenters, Painters and Decorators, Shipwrights, Iron Ship Builders, Caulkers, &c., &c.; and also the Coal Heavers, Ballast-men, Lightermen and their Watchmen. We also appeal to the Public at large for contributions and support on behalf of the Dock Laborers, which may be sent to BEN TILLETT, Great Assembly Hall, Mile End Road; and in doing this we feel sure that our efforts will be appreciated—not as disturbers nor peacebreakers, but as a demand from men determined to swerve not one inch from the attitude they have taken up, to succour the poor and lift up the down-trodden.

On Behalf of the } Amalgamated and United Stevedores { THOS. McCARTHY, *Sec.*
T. M. WILLIAMS, *Sec.*

Members requested to fall into line and to obey Officers in maintaining order.

CONINGHAM BROS., Printers, 797, Commercial Road, Limehouse, E.

LONDON AND INDIA DOCKS JOINT COMMITTEE.

IMPORTANT NOTICE.

Convictions and Imprisonment for Intimidation and Threats.

WHEREAS Dock Labourers and persons employed in the Docks desirous of attending to their lawful employment have been INTIMIDATED and THREATENED and interfered with in the performance of their duties by evil disposed persons inside and outside the Dock premises

NOTICE is hereby given, that several CONVICTIONS have taken place and SEVERE SENTENCES OF IMPRISONMENT passed by Magistrates upon persons who have INTIMIDATED and THREATENED the Dock Labourers and those employed in the Docks.

FURTHER take notice, that on complaint being made to the London and India Docks Joint Committee of any act of INTIMIDATION or THREAT to any of their workmen or persons employed by them the Directors will immediately order THOSE PERSONS INTIMIDATING or THREATENING TO BE PROSECUTED according to law.

By Order,

DOCK HOUSE,
109, Leadenhall Street,
5th September, 1889.

HENRY J. MORGAN,
Secretary.

Charles Skipper & East, Printers, St. Dunstan's Hill, E.C.

Notices issued by the dock unions and dock authorities during the Great Dock Strike of 1889
The dockers' most famous demand was for what became known as 'the docker's tanner' – a 6d per hour rate of pay, a rise of 1d. The strike was one of the key events in 19th-century working-class history and helped to establish a lasting union structure among port workers, which developed in the 20th century into the Transport and General Workers' Union. It drew the general public's attention to the conditions and plight of the urban working class.

Banner of the 'Amalgamated Stevedores Labour Protection League' Branch No. 6, c.1904
The banner commemorates the founding of the Stevedores union after the Great Dock Strike of 1889. The central painted panel shows a London stevedore shaking hands with an Australian 'Wharfie' or port worker. Money sent from Australia secured victory for the strikers.

'Billy and Charley' forgeries, 1857–61
The name Billy and Charley refers to the forgers William Smith and Charles Eaton who began producing fake antiquities in 1857, claiming they had dug them up in Shadwell during the construction of a new dock. Although exposed as forgers, Billy and Charley escaped prosecution and continued to produce and sell such items to unsuspecting buyers until the 1860s.

OPPOSITE:
Henry Thomas Lambert, **1858, George Townsend Cole**
This painting shows the drawing room of a respectable sailmaker living at 307 Wapping High Street, with a view from his window over the river towards Rotherhithe and Bermondsey.

Cut-glass miniature, 1830–35
Carrying a white cameo sulphide portrait of William IV, this was made by Apsley Pellatt's glass manufactory at Blackfriars, close to the river.

Saltglaze stoneware jug, c.1820
This jug, depicting Lord Nelson, was made by Doulton and Watts, Lambeth.

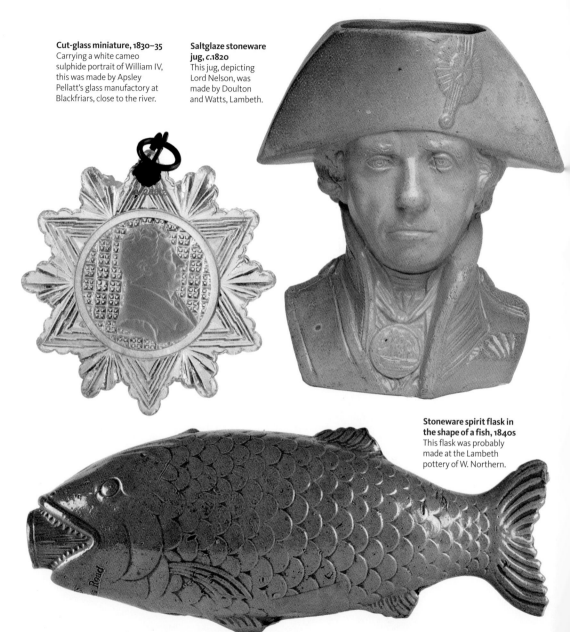

Stoneware spirit flask in the shape of a fish, 1840s
This flask was probably made at the Lambeth pottery of W. Northern.

The pleasure steamer, the *Princess Alice*
The steamer collided with a steam collier off Galleon's Reach at Woolwich in 1878 with the loss of over 640 lives. The published reports of the rescue operation remarked upon the water's smell and the sewage floating in it. It was discovered many had died from poisoning rather than drowning; this point in the river was where untreated sewage was discharged into the river. Illustration from *London Illustrated News*, Saturday 14 September, 1878.

Dock policeman's fog stick, 19th century
Such long sticks were used by PLA policemen to trace the edge of the dock when patrolling during heavy London fogs.

Dock policeman's handcuffs, 1880–1920

Dock policeman's truncheon, 19th century

WAREHOUSE OF THE WORLD 1880–1939

The open quaysides, transit sheds and towering warehouses that lined the docks and riverside housed every conceivable commodity. Here were spices and drugs; grain, sugar, meat and fruit; coffee, cocoa and tea; wines, spirits and tobacco; shells, furs and feathers; leather, skins and hide; timber, paper and jute; wool and oriental carpets, and more. Imports were dominated by Empire produce.

These cargoes were carried to London by a wide variety of ships. In the years 1840 to 1875, sleek and fast 'clippers' were built. Clippers carried tea from China and later, wool from Australia. From 1875, much heavier four-masted 'barques' were built as bulk carriers for wool, grain and nitrate. By the late 1880s, however, steam had overtaken sail.

OPPOSITE:

Unloading cargo
Elevators and electric conveyor belts are used to unload frozen meat from a ship in the Royal Docks, c.1920.
PLA Collection photograph by John H. Avery.

Inspecting cargo
A shipment of Mediterrean sponges are inspected at Cutler Street Warehouses, 1933.
PLA Collection photograph.

Bottle corking machine, 1885–1910
There were extensive wine vaults at the London Docks at Wapping.

Wine labelling bench, 1900–39
The Port of London Authority offered merchants a range of services including wine and spirit bottling and labelling.

Measuring jugs and cans, 1900–30

Tea canister, 1885–1910
Used by a grocer
for storing loose tea
imported from China.

**Carved wooden trade
figures, 19th century**
These figures placed
inside the entrance of a
grocery store would have
indicated that Turkish
coffee and Chinese tea
were sold there.

**Opium pipe confiscated
from a Chinese seaman
in the London Docks,
1875–99**
Opium was smoked by
some of the Chinese
community in Limehouse
and by visiting sailors.

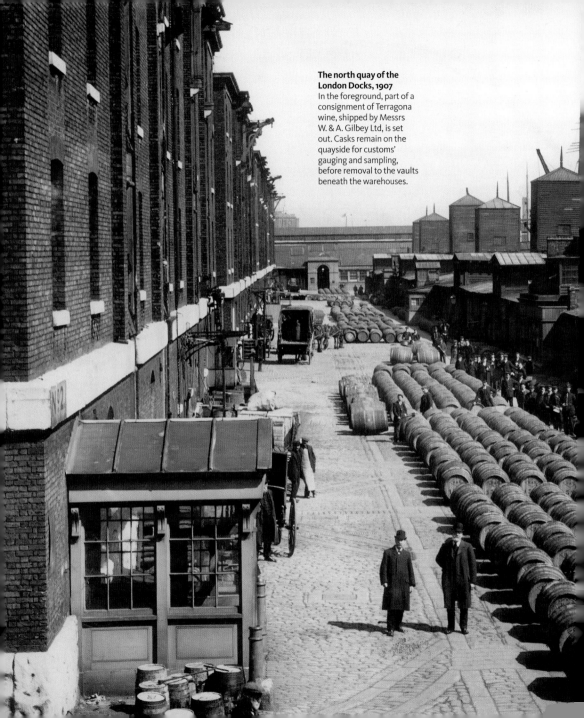

The north quay of the London Docks, 1907
In the foreground, part of a consignment of Terragona wine, shipped by Messrs W. & A. Gilbey Ltd, is set out. Casks remain on the quayside for customs' gauging and sampling, before removal to the vaults beneath the warehouses.

Australian refrigerated mutton being discharged by conveyor from a ship's hold, *c.*1920
PLA collection photograph by John H. Avery.

Tea chests being loaded onto a conveyor at Tilbury Docks, *c.*1920

THAMES LIFE 1930–1940

Boats, barges and tugs were the lifeblood of the port. Hundreds of watermen's skiffs carried passengers, towed rafts of timber, received ships' mooring cables and delivered post to ships in the Pool of London. Familiar with all aspects of craft handling and river currents, watermen, tugmen and lightermen knew the location of all the lock entrances of the docks as well as the hundreds of riverside wharves that lined the Thames.

Waterman's rowing skiff built by Cory's barge works, Charlton, 1920

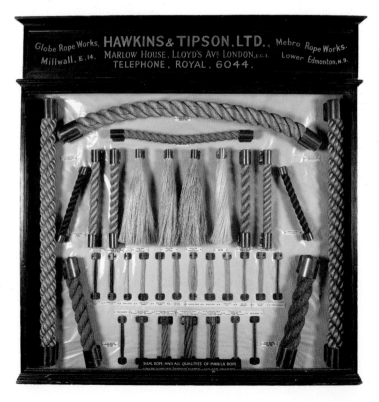

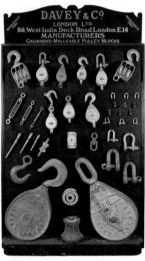

Display of pulleys and shackles, 1920–30
Made by Davey & Co, shipchandlers, West India Dock Road.

Display of rope
Manufactured by Hawkins & Tipson at their Millwall rope factory, 1920.

Model of the Thames sailing barge, *Lily*, 1840–60

Model of the tug, *Mark Lane*, built in 1923
Tugs were used in the port of London to tow ships and lighters in and out of the docks and up and down the river.

Sextant by Henry Hughes and Son, 1882
Presented as a prize to trainee marine officer, Horace Frederick Warne, at the Thames Nautical College, HMS *Worcester*.

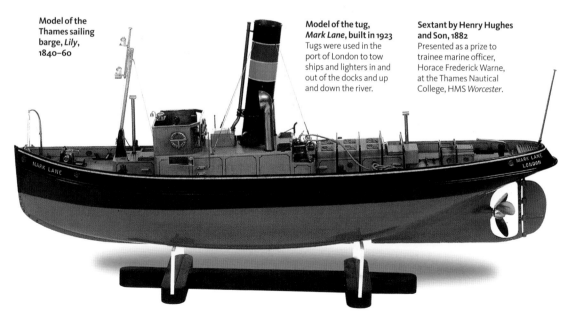

DOCKLANDS AT WAR 1939–1945

The port and its communities bore the brunt of enemy attack during World War Two. They also played a vital part in Britain's fight-back. London tugs, sailing barges and launches assisted in the evacuation of troops from Dunkirk in May 1940. On the afternoon of 7 September 1940 – 'Black Saturday' – the Luftwaffe targeted riverside works and the docks. Fire and smoke from incendiary and high explosive bombs soon silhouetted the river. The Blitz had begun, and continuous night bombing was to last for 13 weeks.

Dockyards and riverside factories, many now employing more women in the workforce, supported the war effort. Tate & Lyle manufactured aeroplane parts as well as refined sugar. Cable works produced much of the Pipe Line Under the Ocean (PLUTO), used to supply fuel oil for the Allied advance from Normandy in 1944. Many of the Phoenix Units of the Mulberry Harbours, used at the Normandy landings in June 1944, were built in the docks and along the river. Over 23,000 vessels and craft were converted, maintained and repaired. Even after victory was in sight, attacks by V1 and V2 rockets brought further destruction to the area in 1944 and 1945.

OPPOSITE:
River Emergency Services' volunteers, 1940
Carrying bandages and blankets, these three volunteers take a break from their civil defence duties to pose for this photograph.

Docklands on fire during the first German mass bombing raid on London, 7 September 1940
The rising palls of smoke mark out the London Docks beyond the Tower of London and Tower Bridge. *PLA Collection photograph.*

Port of London Authority mobile canteen, 1942
During World War Two, dockers worked under difficult conditions unloading ships with the constant threat of an air raid. Mobile canteens supplied them with hot drinks and snacks on the quayside. *PLA Collection photograph.*

Tins of dried milk and eggs imported from the USA, 1940s
Key foodstuffs were rationed during and after the war. Large amounts of tinned goods were imported from the USA. *On loan form the Sainsbury Archive.*

Consul air-raid shelter, c.1940
Designed by PLA engineers to hold up to two adults, these shelters were used by dock policemen and firewardens unable to leave their posts during air-raid attacks.

Casing of an unexploded German bomb that fell on Millwall, 1939–45
In 1941, the basement of Bullivant Wharf, Millwall, was in use as an air-raid shelter. Tragically, bombs fell on the wharf and 44 local people were killed, with a further 60 injured.

PLA Civil Defence warden's helmet and civilian gas mask, 1939–45

The last complete Phoenix Unit or Mulberry Harbour leaves through the King George V entrance, 1944 These floating harbours were essential for D-Day operations.

Model of the Maunsell Forts, 1946 This model shows the forts built to defend the River Thames against attack during World War Two. Positioned along the Thames Estuary, the forts were named after the Civil Engineer, Guy Maunsell, and became the first line of defence against aircraft and mine-laying vessels.

**Winston Churchill visiting
East India Docks, 1944**
*Ministry of Supply
photograph from the
PLA Collection.*

Fireman's axe, 1939–45
Used by a fireman
working at East India
Dock during the Blitz.

George Medal, 1941
Awarded to the PLA Police
Constable, Edward George
Walker, for bravery during
the Blitz.

**Molten cast-iron
warehouse column**
This warehouse column
was melted in the heat
of a fire during the Blitz,
1940.

**Portable magnetic field
telephone, c.1941**
Made by Siemens Brothers'
electrical engineering and
cable factory at Woowich.

The Human Chain, 1940,
William Ware

This painting depicting rescue and
salvage crews at work in a bombed
warehouse captures the devastation
caused by enemy bombing.
Reproduced courtesy of Martin Ware.

NEW PORT, NEW CITY 1945 ONWARDS

Nothing could have prepared local communities for the scale and pace of economic and social change which swept through London's post-war port area. Successfully rebuilt by 1955, much of Docklands was in a state of decline and dereliction by 1975. Plans to regenerate Docklands were hotly contested and its eventual rebirth was hard-won. The opening of new container berths at Tilbury in 1968 sealed the fate of the old up-river docks. Closures began in 1967, and in 1981 even the once mighty Royal Docks group had closed. Wharf, factory and business closures followed. London Docklands Development Corporation (LDDC) was charged in 1981 with the physical, economic and social regeneration of 22 square kilometres (8.5 square miles) of inner London. Docklands' groups fought hard to establish a fair deal for local residents, both campaigning against and working with the LDDC and developers.

Campaign poster, c.1985
Produced by the Docklands Community Project for the Cherry Garden Action Committee, Bermondsey.

Campaign mug, 1986
Issued by the unions during the Wapping dispute between striking printworkers and Rupert Murdoch's News International.

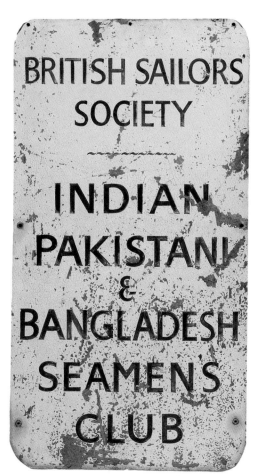

Since 1981, new transport networks, new housing, new businesses and new leisure space have transformed Docklands. Canary Wharf, with its landmark towers, is now London's second business district. Multinational companies now go about their business where ocean-going ships were once docked. The area's multicultural residential mix reflects both its trading past and its trading present. Fittingly, the Port of London remains the country's largest port, although its main activities are now located downriver.

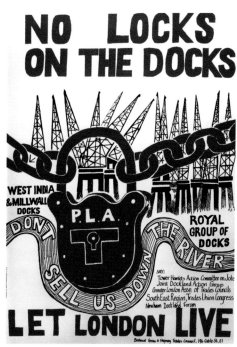

Sign from the British Sailors' Society building at Tilbury Docks, c.1971

No Locks on the Docks **campaign poster, 1970s** Produced by unions and community groups campaigning for the regeneration of the Docklands' area.

RMS *Rangitiki* in the Royal Albert Dock, 1956
The long line of ships moored at the berths on either side of the dock and the numerous lighters support the claim made by lightermen that they were able to 'walk' across the docks.
PLA Collection photograph.

SAINSBURY STUDY CENTRE

Opened in October 2005, the Sainsbury Study Centre is the result of a partnership between the Museum of London and the Sainsbury Archive Trust to open up access to archive collections held at the Museum.

Museum of London Docklands Library & Archives charts the development and activity of the port and Docklands from 1770 onwards. Around 70% of the collection is formed by the Port of London Authority archive. Other collections relate to port and River Thames activities including trades, industrial relations, river management and aspects of Docklands regeneration. There is also a large photographic collection consisting of over 40,000 port-related images.

Branching out
Harry Byford, manager, with his staff at Somers Town branch in 1904. Eggs were usually displayed and sold outside the shop.

Quick dried peas
Packaging from 1971, by the influential company Design Studio. It shows both the old price of 1s 5d and the decimal price of 7p.

Hygenic floors
In early branches, floors were covered in a ceramic mosaic in shades of grey, blue, green, white and brown. The tiles were made by Italian craftsmen employed by Minton Hollins.

The Sainsbury Archive documents the history and development of one of the nation's oldest food retailers from its foundation in London in 1869, as well as providing a unique record of the evolution of the grocery trade and consumer trends. Product packaging and advertising material from the retail stores are particularly well represented within the collection.

These extensive archives include documents, photographs, prints, plans, objects and film and sound recordings. Together they provide a wealth of information for the study of many aspects of social, economic and local history. In the Information Zone, a range of paper and digital information is available for browsing, including collection guides, reference books, photographs and film.

In 2009, new displays from the Sainsbury Archive were added to this area, featuring photographs of some of the earliest London shops, advertising material, staff uniforms and a timeline charting the company's history through product packaging. There is also a Port and River Archives section which includes signed letters from the British Antarctic Expeditions.

The Search Room is open by appointment for visitors who wish to consult original archive material – further information is available from the box office.

MUDLARKS GALLERY

The Mudlarks Gallery is an interactive space for children under 11. It is a fun learning area, where children can explore a variety of activities.

Welcome Zone
- Meet the cartoon characters, Elli Phant and Stevie Dore, who will act as guides
- Sniff the 'smelly pipes'

Early Years Zone
- Enjoy the soft play area, with its climbing frames, chute and Docklands Light Railway Train
- Put together the Docklands' giant jigsaw

Map Zone
- Discover a range of commodities and where they came from

Building Zone
- Construct some of Docklands' landmark buildings
- Touch and match the building finishes used at Canary Wharf

Dock Work Zone

- Meet some of the 'dock people' and the tools of their trades
- See how cargoes were weighed on a beamscale
- Use ropes and pulleys to make light work of lifting
- Balance a clipper ship with cargo

Waterworks Zone

- Tie some of the knots used on ships and in the docks
- Take a look inside the big diving helmets
- See what you can find hidden on the foreshore discovery beach
- Try and spot the real archaeological foreshore finds

MUSEUM OF LONDON

Step inside the Museum of London for an unforgettable journey through the capital's turbulent past. Discover prehistoric London, see how the city changed under the Romans and Saxons, wonder at medieval London and examine the tumultuous years when London was ravaged by civil war, plague and fire. Then venture into the Galleries of Modern London where you can walk the streets of Victorian London, take a stroll in recreated pleasure gardens and marvel at the magnificent Lord Mayor's Coach.

FREE entry

Museum of London
150 London Wall, London EC2Y 5HN

Website: www.museumoflondon.org.uk
Tel: 020 7001 9844
Email: info@museumoflondon.org.uk

Open daily 10am–6pm
(closed 24–26 December)

 St Paul's, Barbican, Moorgate

 Liverpool Street, City Thameslink, Farringdon

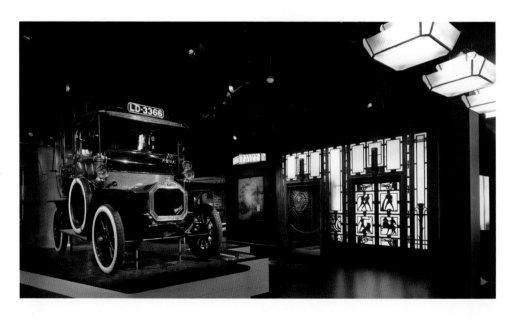

VISITOR INFORMATION

For general information
Telephone 020 7001 9844 or visit
the Museum's website
www.museumoflondon.org.uk/docklands

**Be the first to know about events
and exhibitions**
Have details of events and exhibitions, plus
special offers, sent straight to your inbox by
signing up to receive our free enewsletter.
Visit **www.museumoflondon.org.uk/enews**
or enquire at the information desk during
your visit.

Opening hours
Open daily 10am–6pm
(closed 24–26 December)

Shop
The Museum of London Docklands shop has
something for everyone – from our fantastic
selection of books and DVDs about the docks
and the East End to great gift ideas and pocket-
money toys. If you would like to know more
about our products or services, including our
school goody bag offer, please do not hesitate
to contact us directly at
docklandsshop@museumoflondon.org.uk

**Eating and drinking at
the Museum of London Docklands**
Take a break with a drink, sandwich, salad or
homemade cake in our Museum café
conveniently located on the entrance level.
Our bar restaurant offers a menu based on fresh
seasonal produce and is an ideal place to stop
before or after your visit to the Museum.
For more information about the restaurant
facilities at the Museum, please contact
020 7538 2702 or visit
www.museumoflondon.org.uk/docklands

**Access and facilities for visitors
with disabilities**
The Museum is fully accessible to wheelchair
users. Please call or visit our website to find out
about the services and facilities we provide that
may help you during your visit.

Schools
We offer a rich programme of free sessions,
video conferences and INSET courses for
primary, secondary and special schools to
enrich teaching across the curriculum. See the
Learning section of our website for details.

Family and adult events
From talks, walks and tours to art workshops,
live performances and storytelling, there's
always something happening at the Museum of
London Docklands for both adults and families,
so why not get involved? Visit our website for
the latest events programme or pick up a leaflet
during your visit.

Group visits
With special rates for groups of 10 or more
people on a range of tours, talks and walks, find
out how we can make your group visit a day to
remember on 020 7001 9844.

Ship in King George V dry dock ,1921. *PLA print.*

Picture Library

The Museum of London Picture Library holds thousands of images illustrating the history of London and its people, including many images from the Museum of London Docklands.

An extensive range of prints are available to purchase from **www.museumoflondonprints.com**.

Images are available to license for editorial use from **www.museumoflondonimages.com**.

Please contact the Picture Library for more details on 020 7814 5612/5604, or email **picturelib@museumoflondon.org.uk**

Filming

The Museum buildings and galleries provide a unique location for filming. For details of conditions and fees please contact the Press Office on 020 7814 5502 or email **press@museumoflondon.org.uk**

Host your event at the Museum of London Docklands

The Museum of London Docklands offers exceptional opportunities for corporate entertaining, from formal dinners for up to 130 guests and drinks receptions for up to 800 guests, to daytime and evening meetings and conferences for up to 146 delegates. Please contact the sales team on 020 7001 8816 or email **docklands@museumoflondon.org.uk**

Supporting the Museum of London Docklands

Philanthropy and sponsorship are vital elements in the continuing success and development of the Museum of London Docklands. To discuss ways that you or your company can get involved, please ring the Development Office on 020 7814 5666.

Quayside cranes in the Royal Victoria Dock, 1917. *PLA print.*